Undefined Love

Undefined Love

CLARENCE A. HUBBARD

Charleston, SC
www.PalmettoPublishing.com

Undefined Love

Copyright © 2021 by Clarence A. Hubbard

All rights reserved

No portion of this book may be reproduced,
stored in a retrieval system, or transmitted in any form
by any means–electronic, mechanical, photocopy, recording,
or other–except for brief quotations in printed reviews,
without prior permission of the author.

Paperback ISBN: 978-1-63837-766-5

Table of Contents

Undefined.	1
The First	2
Neglected me.	3
A different lens.	4
Shot clock lover	5
Decision Time	6
Voicemail	7
Text message	8
LOVE	9
LOVE.II.	10
Table for two.	11
A dozen roses..	12
Marriage Vows.	13
Together	14
The Answer.	15
Narrative.	16
The Game.	17
How Could I Ever…	18
If you ever gave me a chance	19
Tell her the truth.	20
Male Ego.	21
Wrong Way.	22
Mirror	23
What we could be.	24
Clean up.	25

Sunrise	26
Who I am	27
Reflection	28
Unspoken Words	29
Don't go	30
Reminisce	31
Without you	32
Dreamer	33
Different type	34
Over-Concerned	35
November	36
Changing	37
Next up	38
Winter Vibe	39
Meant to be	40
Options	41
Before you do	42
You did it	43
Autumn	44
Same female different her	45
Farewell Chapter	46
Undefined season	47
Deep sea attraction	48
Left you there	49
What we had	50
Those nights	51
Valentine's day	52
Closet space	53
Lonely	54
Foregone conclusion	55
Deserve You	56
Transparent	57
To be continued...	58
No more longing	59
Final Page	60

Undefined

Our love is unclear,
rumors about us swirl from ear to ear,
we contemplate our feelings wondering if their pure.
We both feel the need to be pleased but not by one another,
We're infatuated by each other
but unmotivated to be together.
Our love is strange and hard to explain,
There are many things I could say but it wouldn't make our
love any less deranged.
You're somewhat like a rental waiting to be exchanged,
My heart is overwhelmed by blurry emotions,
A love like this is undefined with no clear-cut design.

The First

You were the first one,
You were the fist one to show me what real love was,
You were the first one to show me
how a true lady should act,
Your head was on straight not allowing
any insults to get in your way,
You were the first one to make me feel like a man…
You let me take control,
But that's how I lost you…
Feeling superior, now there's no you…
And all I have is myself.

Neglected me.

You neglected me …
Then questioned me but yet I still didn't see the plot…
But the setting was set to effect and reject me,

You neglected me…
Then departed away from me…
Felt like my heart got snatched from me,
you left me with a gaping hole,
Emotions spiraling out of control,
I don't want to love again...
Because of fear…
And this story being told…

You neglected me,
Leaving me speechless and defenseless…
I was overwhelmed with emotion …
My heart started to erode while my mind gravitated out…
No such thing as love anymore…
She seemed to have moved out.

A different lens

I speak for the voiceless,
The ones who question love,
The ones who question their future.

I speak for the ones who feel judged, who are judged,
I speak for the ones who are anti-social
and are full of emotions,
I speak for the ones who wanna shine bright
like a star in the sky,
I speak for the ones who deal with heart break,
hoping it will beat and form as one,
I speak for the discouraged, hoping to gain courage.
I speak for the voiceless,
I speak for myself,
The voiceless.

Shot clock lover

Only ten seconds left,
That's enough time for me to express this love
that I have deep down inside for you.
Eight seconds remain,
For me to tell you my truth and reveal all of the dirt
and gilt that comes from my past.
Six seconds more,
Time that you take away to deal with and absorb all
the things I gave to you based off the words I just spoke.
The seconds dwindle down to four,
Nothing more for me to give to you or hold back .
Just two seconds left,
Left for both of us to make a decision on whether or not
we really want to stay committed.

Text message

It says delivered,
But I don't know if it really got through to you,
Text Message…
My messages come up in blue
while your responses come up in grey,
We constantly make minimum conversation
like "Hey" or "Wassup"
To me that's not enough,
Text Message…
You must have some one else in your contacts that has
your attention,
Because you don't reply anymore
Text message…

LOVE

Love is essential,
Breath taking,
It is commitment and longevity,
Love is a two-way street,
Love is you and me.

Love is, the gratitude that I show in my attitude
whenever I'm around you,
Love is sacrifice,
Patience,
Dedication.

Love is the shoulder I lend you to cry
on in a time of grievance,
Love is the helping hand I give you when you need it.

Love is the birth of something new,
It's like a newborn baby that was given to you,
So dull and precious.

LOVE.II

Love is truthless, and ruthless,
Love is supposed to be a pact between two,
Love can be misleading,
And leave one's soul bleeding,
Love is unpredictable, but one's choice can be predictable,

Love causes emotions which can spiral out of control,
But can also take its toll,
Love is an achievement,
But it always finds away to leave someone
in a state of grievance,
Love is unpredictable…
But one's choices can be predictable…

Table for two

I couldn't believe my eyes,
It was me and you sitting at a table for two…
Talking and laughing, enjoying our time…
You, so hardworking loving your grind,
You, not easy to define,
Me, so amused by you seeing your beauty,
Such a joy,
Sitting at that table what an amazing time…
I couldn't believe my eyes,
I wasn't surprised by who I was talking to,
I was speaking to a queen,
A young lady with dreams…
A queen…
Just me and you at a table for two engaged in conversation,
A wonderful night no desperation or confrontation,
A wonderful night amazed by you…
The one and only …
A queen...
A wonderful night such a beautiful thing.

A dozen roses.

A dozen roses…
A dozen roses that'll never be sent,
to a lovely lady that will one day feel the feeling of repent,
no sinning involved just regret from decisions,
A dozen roses that'll never be sent to her
for the simple fact that she's not the one,
The one for me,
A dozen roses…
A dozen roses that'll never be sent
because love is not being met,
The heart is feeling upset,
They both have feelings that neither one can protect,
A dozen roses…

Marriage Vows

One day…
One day we'll meet,
Meet at the altar,
We'll meet in front of a group,
A group that holds expectations,
For me,
For you,
For us,
One day…
One day you'll question me,
You'll question me wondering if my feelings still remain the same.
One day…
One day I'll hold you while you carry our offspring,
Our everything,
Our flesh and blood,
Our creation,
Through love and not fornication.
One day…
One day we'll meet,
Meet at the end…
And be taken away…
One day…

Together

Loving you feels different,
Every split second I'm with you,
Your eyes reassure me of my confidence.

As I look into your eyes,
You shed a tear,
Your tear falls onto my shirt like paint splatting onto a canvas,

Loving you feels like an unrealistic chance,

I'm positioned to be in your possession for a long time,

If loving you was a crime,
I'd constantly commit.

The Answer

How do I tell you that I love you
without overstepping my boundaries?
I don't even know if you're into that,
I hope you are because that would truly heal my heart…
And these emotions that I'm going through,
But what if you're not…
Do I have to keep living in the gloomy days that await me,
Or do I just step away completely?
I hope you are the answer…
I've been looking for.

Narrative

You wanna change the narrative so bad,
That it hurts you when I do right,
I see myself with another girl because…
She might have the potential to further me to new heights,

You wanna change the narrative so bad,
That you can't even see what you're causing,
If anyone were to love you again that would be daunting,
Your emotions are quick to boil and spill over,
Loving you was hard because
you always wanted to take over and manage,
Now look at your new situation…
He leaves you stranded,
I guess what you wish for always becomes granted.

The Game.

You were the only one I made time for,
You were my first love and passion,
Nothing could ever change my feelings for you,
No girl could come between us,
The struggles we had,
The moments we had after,
A loss and even during a win,
The feeling of you in my hands,
Whether I pass or keep you for myself,
I would slam you against the hard wood,
Out of frustration,
But you bounced back up to keep me,
Focused and dedicated,
Me and you…
Became good at one thing,
And that was getting to the line…
A matter of fact, that's were we spent most of our time,
Seeing you depart from my hands and praying you'd go in,
You're such a beaty when I see you back spin,
No girl can come between us…
But it seems that time has,
I don't know about our future, but I loved our past.

How Could I Ever...

You expect me to love you after how you did me,
You did me wrong all along you knew we could never be,
You played me degraded me knowing you wouldn't claim me,
Now I sit here a free agent with a heart that's tainted along
with feelings that have been mistaken,
You expect me to be okay with this broken heart knowing
that I can't restart and get back on the right path,
You showed me what love was then...
I became so attached... not to you...
But to your love.

If you ever gave me a chance

I don't want to be your last resort and most definitely don't
want our love to feel forced,
I rather see you smiling bit upset feeling
like you made a bad choice,
I don't wanna be in your way but I wanna be where you are,
I want to be stuck in your presence
but never feeling depression,
I want to be the man they can take you further in life,
making you my potential wife,
I wanna do it big…
but I don't want to be your last resort even though
I'm willing to put you first,
love is so commercial while our hearts don't know
what they want…
so, they rather deal with the heart than trusting one
another to find his true worth.

Tell her the truth

Only reason I stall is because I'm afraid to give you my all,
I don't want to give you half because it won't seem right…
I knew love was real when you crossed my sight,
I never felt love especially the way you give it out,
it's like an addiction which has been conflicted and
wondering and hoping for a way out
it's not you it's clearly me,
falling in love just isn't my cup of tea,
I'm a man that runs from commitment which shouldn't be,
half of me loves you while the other half is undecided,
you shouldn't be with a man especially
when his heart is so divided.

Male Ego

I love you so much to the point where I cheat…
I cheat because I have to, I cheat because I'm a man
I'm a man a man who runs from my problems I run from
you knowing you won't understand my pain…
I'm a man that runs from you to her looking for
satisfaction and understanding…
I'm a man.
a man with insecurities…
a man with no morals…
I'm a man.
a man with no guidance…
nor structure…
nor am I ready to mature…
I'm a man.

Wrong Way

For some reason I always end up making
a left turn on memory Rd.
I can't figure out why I want to be with you after all the
stuff we went through,
Is it your amazing qualities or the beauty that I saw in you?
Something continues to pull me back in towards you,
Is if you were the last female on earth…
I wouldn't mind a reconnection…
But I no longer have the ability to give you…
love and affection.

Mirror

Trying to become the man I mirror is
the hardest thing in life…
finding a queen to be by my side…
can I ever call her my wife?
I've been terrorized by my creator which has led me to
follow in his steps…
one parent in the home so it's even harder to mirror this
man…

What we could be

What we could be
we could be the sand to the beach…
the land of the free
we could be the icing on the cake…

we could be the main attraction,
after all you were the one who had me attracted…
we could be the definition of love…
we can be the wrinkles in the sheets…
an attention grabber of a speech
we could be a farfetched dream that can't be reached…
what we could be.

Clean up.

Looking for you in the shadow of my mistakes
wanting you to just take the wheel and steer this ship…
bad decision back-to-back is became a habit…
I'm human but lack common sense and that's why I so desperately need you…
looking for you in the shadow of my mistakes…

Sunrise

I have to see the sunrise…
seen way too many people demise…
I like to see the sunrise…
it helps me stay in tune with life…
the sunrise flows up high in the Sky…
waiting for me to come look at it eye to eye.
sunrise…

Who I am

I continue to find myself out of bounds,
outdated, complacent, and impatient...
I question why but nothing arises,
no more falling in love because I'm tired of seeing that she
got other plans that revolve with another man,
no, I'm not the bitter type or the Twitter type or the one
that gets on IG and helps your pics get 100 likes,
I'm a different type maybe a prototype,
but while I find myself out of bounds,
I contemplate them regenerate...
as I tell myself that all those past mistakes created
who I am today
and that life goes on rather than stop and wait.

Reflection

If I shall change, I'm doing it for myself,
If I remain then you shall choose somebody else,
If I shall lay it should be with you,
If I shall cheat it should be worth the moment,
If we fight let it be out of love and not anger,
If I shall die don't release a tear, nor try to save me,
let the death of me be a rebirth of someone new and improved.

Unspoken Words

Unspoken words
words that are never said nor mentioned…
words that I say that will never get your attention,
words that would bring us together
and hopefully make us last forever,
words that are never said nor mentioned…
unspoken words …
words that are bitter in somewhat sweet,
words that can get you swept off your feet,
words that will have you questioning me,
words that will fill up your head with lies,
words that will constantly keep you up at night wondering
if what was said was truly right,
words that are never said nor mentioned…
unspoken words…

Don't go

You can do what you want,
leave me,
just know that I won't stop loving you,
I'm gonna love you harder…
I'm gonna love you as if we were still together,
latched on like a magnet…
you can leave just know it's gonna drive me crazy,
having my mind filled with "what if" scenarios,
blaming myself for your early exit
as if you didn't plan on it earlier,
you can do what you want,
you can leave me,
but I prefer you to stay,
stay lay be by my side keep hope alive,
be the end of my night,
the sunrise to the blue Sky
you can leave me,
just know I won't stop loving you.

Reminisce

Damn...
why do they make me feel like it's my fault...
it's kind of crazy that our conversations reached a halt,
I guess that's what happens when the season starts to turn to fall,
no text not even a call
an ostracized relationship keeps putting my heart on froze,
neither one of us even knows where this thing should go
I rather just be alone, far away from you,
because every time I look at you, I see a narcissistic chick
who can't manage to tell the truth getting caught in your
web like your name is Charlotte,
no longer want to be a part of you because your love comes
with a lot of precautions like they have on the back of the
liquor bottles that you intake,
taking it to the head as if you had a stressful day seeing you
in a new frame of mind always comes to mind,
but you gave up on me like you ran out of time,
but I fight to get an hour back
because our love has strings attached,
Damn...
why do they make me feel like it's my fault...
it's kind of crazy that our conversations reached a halt
I guess that's what happens
when the season starts to turn to fall,
no text not even a call
for you I would have risked it all.

Without you

I won't feel complete if I can't wake up next to you,
smelling your morning breath as you roll over and smiled
telling me good morning,
when I tell you, I love you not to interrupt you, but to
show you how serious I am about being with you,
I would feel less than if I couldn't cuddle you in my arms,
watching the sun go down at the mosquitoes start to suck
on our skin as we give a quick glance at each other feeling
like we are meant to be,
I'd rather be obsessed and crazy over you then…
single and broke…
I'd rather be the guy that brings you love and hope
then the one who name calls and provokes,
I want to love you and no one else.

Dreamer

I wish the nights came quicker…
I wish love wasn't found through pictures,
I wonder if hearts were meant to be bitter
or even broken in some cases,
I judge love with no patience,
I judge her off her past relations…
knowing life is full of revelations defined by two, who have
different expectations but still motivated by temptation,
which becomes the ultimate sacrifice,
I wish the nights came quicker…
I wish being rich wasn't the big picture,
I wish Alcoholics would put down the hard liquor
and the spritzers,
I wonder if money will become an independent variable
one day…
I question when I'll stop being dumbfounded
by what they say,
knowing that there's truth in some lies,
living life through others and disguised.

Different type

I don't know…
I mean…
I guess…
it was crazy never thought I'd meet you…
meet you…
a different type… opposite of shallow…
I'm glad we met up.
Continue…
let's continue our enriching dialogue…
let's create a prelude …
let's be together me and you…
let's define each other…
let's unravel each other …
let's devour each other …
I'm thinking out loud again…
a different type… opposite of shallow…
I don't know…
I mean…
I guess

Over-Concerned

Am I too content in life,
am I meant to have a wife, or am I way too contrite,
constantly wondering if I'm doing things just right,
what if my future is not bright like the ring that goes on
her finger after she agrees to marry,
what if it's dark like a November night,
what if I'm never accepted and constantly rejected,
what would I do,
would you be there for me to run to?

November

November…
That's when leaves get brighter and the winds get colder,
but most of all a drunk mind fails to become sober…
November…
It's when hearts start to break…
and love seems to be a mistake and people become easier to replace…
November…
It's when apples get picked off of trees by kids who looked like me and you…
When we were younger…
November…
It's when I wanna be alongside you…
With all that we went through…
November…

Changing

Things change, I guess that's how it goes…
Our love started to drift apart; our love became faded…
Our good times remain in the dark…
I went ghost …
You pushed me back…
No longer could feel you up close…
My beds empty since you decide to leave…
"I keep fucking up"
That's one of my biggest pet-peeves…
"I keep pushing for love"
Instead of allowing it to come to me…
"I'm broken-hearted"
But I'm the one to blame…
"What about restarting and going back to the basics"
She's looking for love and you…
Are an easy replacement.

Next up

How can I cheat and break your heart…
when I've been there before…
You're the one I love,
Why turn to another when we were meant for each other…
Why would I put you through hell…
Why would I make you feel the need
to regret being with me…
I'm not your ex…
I'm just next…
The one who wants to keep you from feeling upset,
I'm just next…
The one who wants to see you do your best,
I'm next…
The one who wants to feel your effect…
How could… I cheat…
Commit a sin in my eyes…
How could I break your heart,
When I've been there before…
Why break your heart when I'm still there.

Winter Vibe

The winters getting quicker my purpose is getting thinner
than the wool sheets that I find myself confined in,
which means my space is restricted,
no space to think which leaves me conflicted,
opening new wounds while the old ones
haven't completely healed yet,
what are the consequences of my actions if I don't do right,
what would life be like,
who am I to remain uptight,
what's life really like when you don't think twice,
what's an opportunity to an opportunist,
what school to a person that's clueless,
no guidance or true influence
what's a lie to her she ain't stupid,
I'd give her the world plus Jupiter,
the winters coming quicker,
my purpose is getting thinner.

Meant to be

I've seen god take many but he still left you,
He left you with me so we could plant that seed and live life,
Until we turn it over to eternity,
We could be what they mistakenly don't want to see,
Like the man will ever view me in the lens of equality,
I regardlessly harp on the idea of my currency
purchasing a wedding ring,
That'll leave us both looking like more than a fling…
Who cares if they become jealous, greed will never achieve,
That's like me snatching my heart back
since you decided to cheat,
Don't put your hand out thinking it'll be easy to retrieve,
I'm stuck in my way I'm feeling less and less complete,
I've seen god take many but the still left…
Me.

Options

That's what you said…
You told me you had options,
I'm no longer worth your time because you have
Options…
I'm not number one or even four,
You pushed me to the side and hit ignore,
I wanted your love but you chose to explore,
I wanted the key to your heart,
But you didn't want me to be the one to open that door,
You played me like a PS5,
You kept up your magnificent lies,
You made my healthy heart die,
Your love was like a job,
And all I did was apply…
You chose your options over me,
No, us that'll never be,
I loved you…but you treated me like glass…
You looked right… through.

Before you do

Please don't break my heart,
I get tired of hitting restart
as soon as I become attached, I don't want to be broken apart,
I was kicked to the curb way too many times,
I keep looking for love but it's seemingly undefined,
"will it come when I hit my prime"
what is love, is it a four-letter word or a mutual feeling
is it used for healing or is just tossed around …
Please don't break my heart,
I get tired of hitting restart, just to be broke down into parts …

You did it

She…
You didn't create on your own, but he's gone,
You say you can do it alone,
You…
Raised in a single parent home…
But didn't think you were going to be left to raise an xy chromosome,
Two thoughts arise…
Abort the mission or start a new tradition…
A baby boy young and gifted…
Near your heart where he should be…
Help him grow like a seed to a tree…
You didn't create on your own… but you're left to raise…
A man alone…
No, it won't be easy, but nothing ever is,
Look at his face as he holds a chuckle and a grin…
Holly people say you made him in sin…
But the only thing that matters is that you…
She…
Love him from within.

Autumn

It was the scent that brought me closer to you…
That sweet fall cherry blossom…
Your eyes a light brown…
Bringing me back to the time I had a fling out of town…
It was the dialect for me…
Teaching me things…
Showing me more…
Giving me you heart, while we entered a new door…
That look you gave me is what had me sold…
You…
The one I want to hold…
You…
The one I want to lose control with…
But it was the name that put things in retrospect…
The cherry blossom…
The out-of-town fling…
It was you…
<u>Autumn</u>…

Same female different her

A heart isn't a heart when it's torn apart…
Love isn't love when she's not willing to play her part…
We were never one from the very start…
A tear falls, not from you but from I…
The one who is like glass… see through…
The one who never seen love … more like abuse…
You're the one I wanted…
The one I didn't get…
The one that never gave me a chance to show my potential… like a second-round draft pick…
You considered me to be below average…
Not enough…
But it wasn't just you…
It was all of them…

Farewell Chapter

They always questioned how we would end…
I simply replied… we're not chapter ten…
We're not a script there's no writing us off…
They want us far apart…
No holding hands… no weekends fully planned…
They always questioned how we would end…
I simply replied… "we can't" …
There's no chance we would split…
Then it happened…
They questioned again… but then…
I simply replied…
"She fell far a different end" …

Undefined season

I wanted you out of desperation…
I couldn't admit it…
I had no preparation…
Now I sit with an open heart not knowing where to start…
I thought you could change that empty feeling
I desperately had inside…
While it still remains, you're the only one that leaves my
mind filled…filled with wanting you…
I wanted you out of desperation…
I wanted you without a reason,
I thought it would be for completion…but
I only find love during the undefined seasons.

Deep sea attraction

It was you…
The one by the sea…
That cup in your hand… fresh smelling green tea…
A beauty…
Making me drop to my knee's as if I we're asking the lord for forgiveness…
Plea after plea…
It was you…
The one by the sea…
No defined look, but the one that could be…
That lockdown finger was seen with no ring…
I could make you the one… no longer mainstream…
It was you…
The one by the sea…
The one I could love no matter the reach…
No verbal words spoken not even a speech… no longer needing to wait…
Because the waves…
Took us deep…

Left you there

I left you there… standing in the rain,
I did it for a reason… it was time to change
so I walked away from your mistreatment…
No longer looking for top of the line…
I just want something decent,
Love is undefined I've been noticing that as of recent,
Just like a car they'll never buy all they do is lease it…
I left you there…
Hoping you'd realize that I'm serious this time, no longer waiting on you to make that decision...
We all need guidance when we run from our intuition.

What we had

I don't know what else I could say…
I don't know what would keep you from going…
Say I get hit with a stray… would you love me more or less…
Knowing the potential of me fading away,
Would it take you to our old days…
Or would you forget them completely…
I still can't manage the thought or the action of you…
Deleting me…
It was a struggle for you and I…
It was like a blossoming rose bush…
That always finds a way to die…
No water or sun could fix what we had…
We're just two independent lovers…
Fast forwarding through the past…

Those nights

What does a long night remind you of?
Does it take you to sleepless nights…?
Where all you do is have thoughts that are incomplete…
Do you ever sit up and think about you and…me?
Does a long night force you to drink?
Do the pillows still leave imprints of me…?
What does a long night remind you of?
Does it speak or is it quiet?
Does it take you to the blogs where everyone is bias?
What does a long night remind you of?
Does it bring you peace?
Or does it want me back where I used to sleep.

Valentine's day

Valentine's day that's what they call it…
A day where money gets spent,
lust turns to love just so hearts can feel fixed…
still forgetting that you're not the only one
they're spending time with…
love that's what they call it…
but it's really just a figure of speech
how can you love each other when all you do is find
yourself tangled in sheets…
just to realize you still incomplete…
Valentine's Day is what they call it…
roses and chocolate is what gets purchased…
till a couple days later when she tells you
"it's just not working"

Closet space

Empty...
it was red lipstick smeared across the mirror...
it was noted that you would be leaving me...
leaving me alone...
no more fresh smelling leather...
no more lavender soap suds falling from the tub...
no more you...
I can still envision you...
envision you applying your extra accessories,
whether it were eyeliner or the shadow
it's the mirror...
the mirror is where you left your mark...
picture after picture that was your work of art...
only thing that remains from you is this message...
it's as clear and pure as the foundation you would put on...
empty...
that's what you leave me with...
empty...
empty closet space...

Lonely

Eight O'clock,
Standing on the balcony…
Lonely…
No one there to console me…
Comfort me…at a time where I need you…
Lonely…
That's how I feel after everything you told me…
I can't believe I lied, that's the old me…
Off… that's how they wrote me…
Lonely…
No clear direction of where I'm going…
Lonely…
I'm back in the past, stuck in the old me…
Lonely…

Foregone conclusion

Where does it end…
better yet when did it ever start…
what is the true meaning behind feelings that you can't feel?
how does it end…
better yet how did it ever start?
why was I ever given the ability to feel…feel such feelings
that don't exist…
when will it end…?
when will this feeling ever make a reasonable contribution
to my livelihood?
again…
where does it end…
how does it end…
when will it end…
when will love be apart…?
instead of unseen and in the dark…

Deserve You

Do I deserve you?
When it comes to love... I feel like I need to reserve you...
Without you there is no love to turn to...
Apart of me feels that I need to earn you...
Rather than yearn for you...
I have this burning feeling inside me...
Like 1942...
Do I deserve you...
When it comes to you...
Can I learn you through and through...
Being apart of your future, creating something new...
Do I deserve you?
Someone so accomplished...
And well put together...
Someone I want to call my forever...
Do I deserve you...

Transparent

Where does my heart lie?
hopefully in the palm of my hands…
hoping you can still feel it beating until it ends…
where does my heart lie?
right next to mine would have been the correct response
but time has passed turning you into ash
where does my heart lie?
it lies with me until we meet again…
something like eternity…
I took a one-way trip to the heavenly gates just to hold
your heart one more time…
you asked…
where does my heart lie?
this time I replied…
"high in the Sky with the Lord by your side" …

To be continued...

To be continued…
That's what we told them…
They made assumptions…
That started to control us…
To be continued…
That's what we agreed to say…
To be continued…
Let's figure it out…
Let's move away and start over again…
Let us find out what life is really about…
To be continued…
That's what we agreed to say…
To be continued…
That's what we wanted…
To be continued…
Seemed cliché…
To be continued…
But you walked away…

No more longing

Every time we're together we want to turn it into forever…
we still have nights where we periodically
stay with one another…
but while we lay…
we question it…
we question if we love each other…
we have mutual interest…
but neither one of us wants to break that cycle…
that cycle… more like a habit…
the type of habit that will have you needing therapy…
neither one of us are aspiring to be apart…
no more longing…
something we both want to escape…
we want to disappear in the comfort of each other…
rather than getting involved with another…
no more longing
let's commit…
instead of loving
wrongful

Final Page.

The last time I wrote… it was about you…
I wrote it to see…
see if you would go for it…
go for my style…
I did it to see if you would actually acknowledge me…
this time it's different...
this is the final page…
this is the page…
the page that I used to vent…
vent everything I've been holding back…
leaving nothing unwrapped…
letting the bruises show…
this is the final straw…
hoping that I won't repeat…
repeat the same struggles…
this is the page…
the page that I don't plan to…
revisit.

To: Lizzie,

I hope that you really enjoy I hope that at some point I'm able to put together [Pt.2] I just hope that you enjoy reading this book of poems, poetry is what explains me as a person it simply defines me.

Ig: C.hubbard_Poetry

7/1/23